MY THIRD
MUSIC THEORY BOOK

Lina Ng

© RHYTHM MP SDN. BHD.1986
U.S. Edition: 2010

Published by
RHYTHM MP SDN. BHD.
1947, Lorong IKS Bukit Minyak 2, Taman IKS Bukit Minyak,
14100 Simpang Ampat, Penang, Malaysia.
Tel: +60 4 5050246 (Direct Line), +60 4 5073690 (Hunting Line)
Fax: +60 4 5050691
E-mail: rhythmmp@mphsb.com
www.rhythmmp.com

Cover Design by
Lim Wai Fun

ISBN 10: 967 98560 7 0
ISBN 13: 978 967 98560 7 1
Order No.: MPM-3002-03US

 # CONTENTS

 My

PAGE ... TITLE

artkoh

My  **3**

Name the notes and rests.

1 _____	4 _____	7 _____
2 _____	5 _____	8 _____
3 _____	6 _____	9 _____

Write the time signatures. | 2/4 | 3/4 | 4/4 |

1. [ ] ♩ 𝄽 ♩

2. [ ] ♫ ♩

3. [ ] ♩ 𝄽 ♩

4. [ ] ♩. ♫

Color the crabs according to the number of counts.

COUNTS	COLOR
1	RED
2	BLUE
3	GREEN
4	YELLOW

How many members are there in each family?

Red Family   - _____ members

Blue Family   - _____ members

Green Family - _____ members

Yellow Family - _____ members

Add bar-lines and name the notes.

A

Write the time signature and the counts.

Complete each measure with

MERRY CHRISTMAS

Hurray! It is Christmas again!

Look at all the presents.

Can you find a box for each item?

Number them in the circles, like this. ②

Put an **X** on the wrong note.

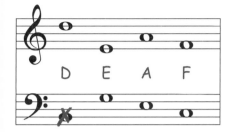

D E A F

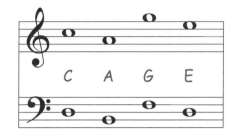

C A G E

B A B E

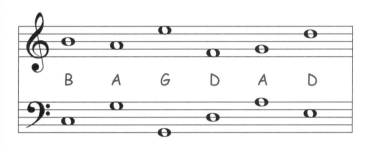

B A G D A D

D E C A D E

Write the letter-names and then write the notes 1 octave lower in the bass.

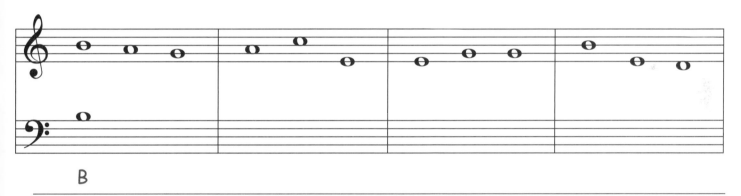

B

Write the letter-names and then write the notes 1 octave higher in the treble.

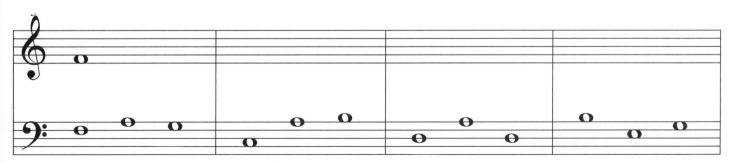

F

Fill in the blanks with the correct answers.

1. This is the _ _ _ _ _ _ clef.

2. This is the _ _ _ _ clef.

3. The _ _ _ _ _ consists of five lines.

4. A _ _ _ joins notes of the same pitch.

5. A _ _ _ _ _ raises a note 1 half step in pitch.

6. A _ _ _ _ lowers a note 1 half step in pitch.

7. A _ _ _ _ _ _ _ restores a note to its original pitch.

8. A _ _ _ _ _ _ _ _ _ _ _ _ has 1 count.

9. A _ _ _ _ _ _ _ _ _ has 2 counts.

10. These are _ _ _ _ _ _ .

BLACK KEYS

Write the letter-names on the white keys.

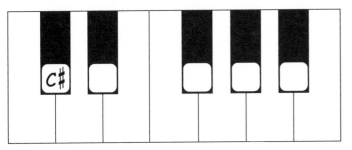

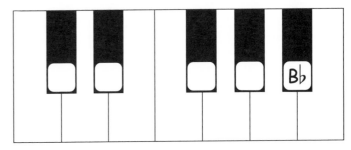

Name the black keys as sharps (♯)

Name the black keys as flats (♭)

Write the letter-names on the white keys and shade the stated key black.

HALF STEP - HIGHER

My ✌

Fill, in the empty boxes, notes that are a half step higher.

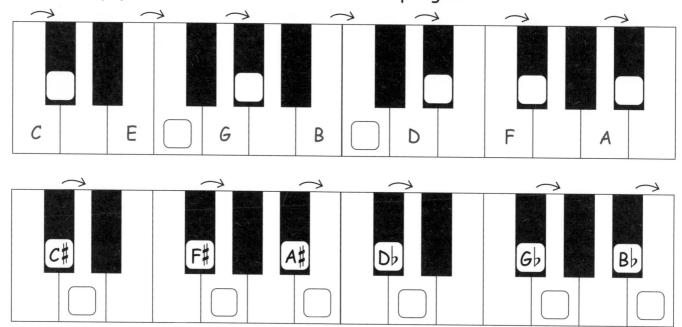

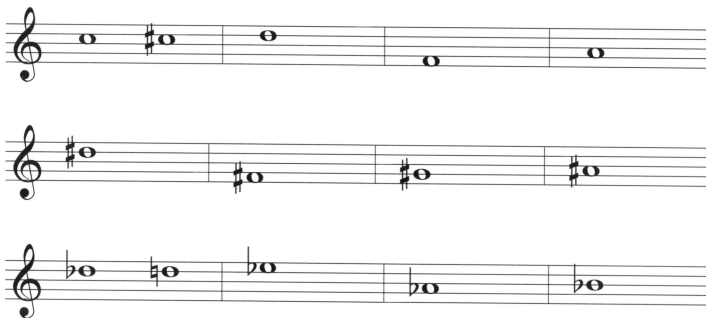

Try these exercises on the keyboard.

Teacher plays a note and student plays the note that is a half step higher.

After each note, write a note that is a half step higher.

My

HALF STEP - LOWER

Fill, in the empty boxes, notes that are a half step lower.

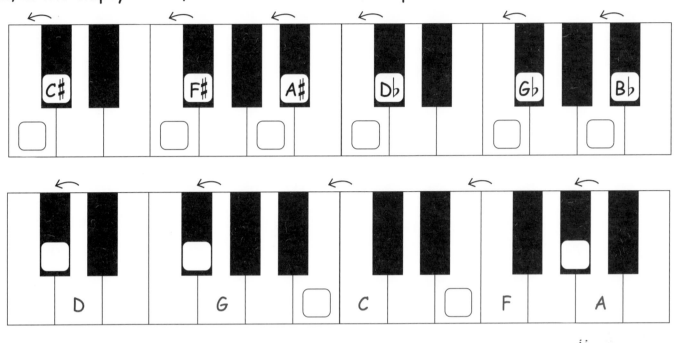

After each note, write a note that is a half step lower.

 # WHOLE STEP – HIGHER / LOWER My

Fill, in the empty boxes, notes that are a whole step higher.

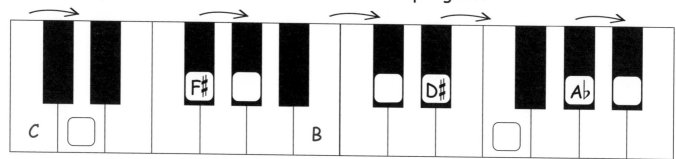

After each note, write a note that is a whole step higher.

Fill, in the empty boxes, notes that are a whole step lower.

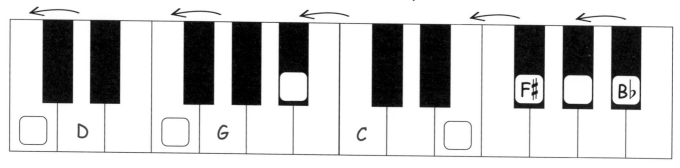

After each note, write a note that is a whole step lower.

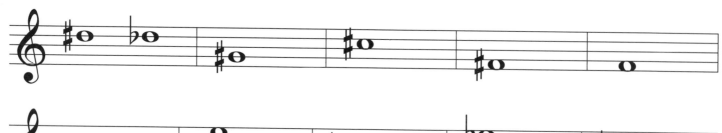

My 🎵 **HIGH SCHOOL TEST**

This is a High School Test. Mark (✔) or (✗) below each measure. Fill in the points scored. Write the names, from highest to lowest scorer.

1) _____   3) _____

2) _____   4) _____

To know the names of the sisters, spell the names of the brothers from right to left.

Half step higher

AZIL / 5

Half step lower

/ 5

Whole step higher

ABE / 5

Whole step lower

/ 5

DOTTED NOTES

The dot increases the length of the note by $\frac{1}{2}$ its original value.

Example:

Complete each measure with

My

  15

Write the counts.

Write the time signatures.

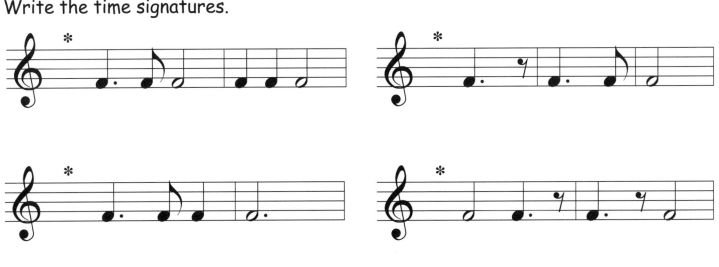

Complete each measure with  or

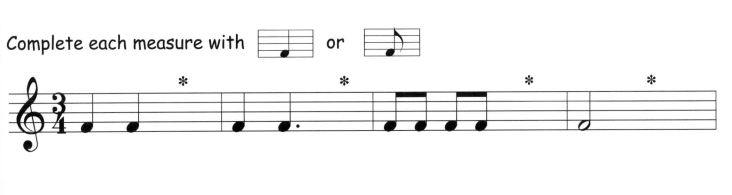

BEAUTY CONTEST

This is a Beauty Contest. Who do you think will walk away with the crown? Take a walk yourself by using the route ☐

The winner is _____ .

KEY SIGNATURES

C major	-	none
G major	-	F♯
F major	-	B♭

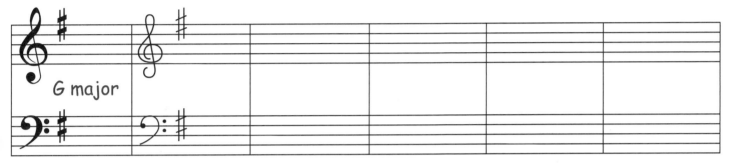

G major

F major

Write the time signature and name the key.

Key _____

Key _____

Key _____

Add accidentals (♯ or ♭) to indicate the keys.

G major

F major

G major

F major

Add bar-lines and name the key.

Key _____

Key _____

LOST ITEMS

Please help Benji, Tanny and Carmen find their belongings (key signatures).
Once you have found them, decide on the key (C, F or G major) and fill it in the
blank spaces provided.

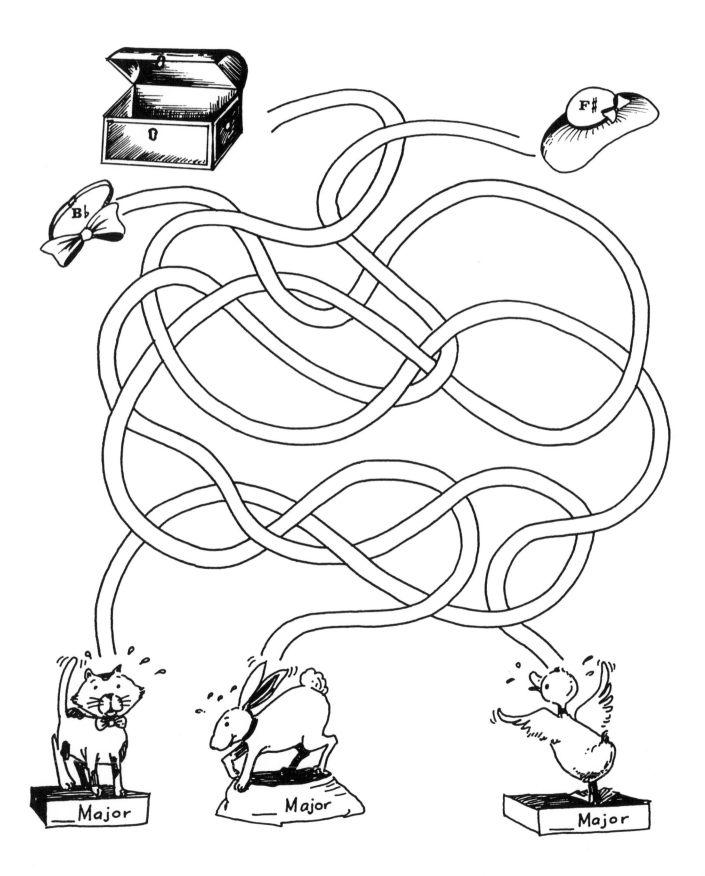

SCALES

My ✌

Write the scales and slur the half steps.

C major

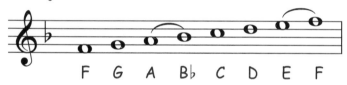

C D E F G A B C

G major

G A B C D E F♯ G

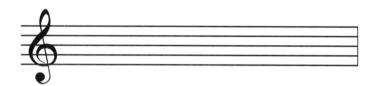

F major

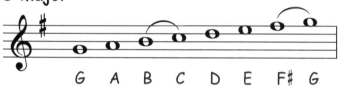

F G A B♭ C D E F

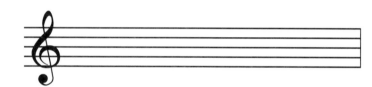

C major

C D E F G A B C

G major

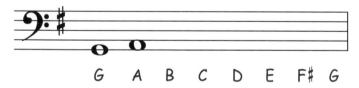

G A B C D E F♯ G

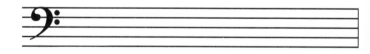

F major

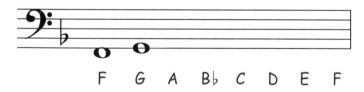

F G A B♭ C D E F

(NOTE: Teacher should demonstrate on the keyboard and explain the half steps, before student attempts this section.)

Write the scales and then color the notes that you would play.

Remember to write the key signature and slur half steps.

C major

G major

F major

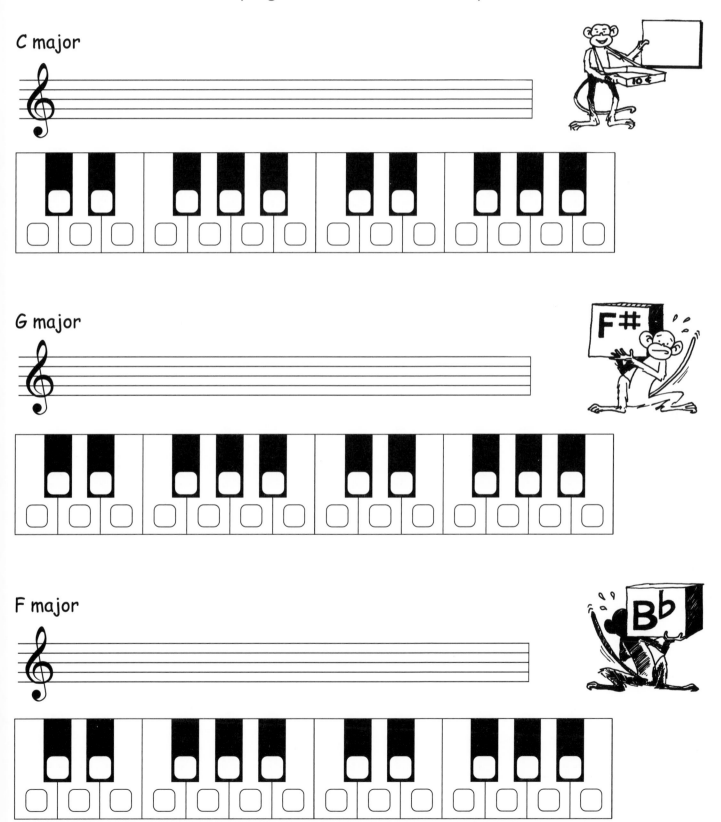

My 🎵

Write the scales and then color the notes that you would play.
Remember to write the key signature and slur the half steps.

C major

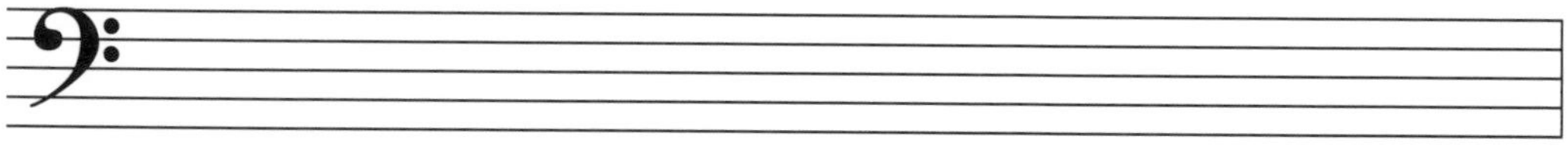

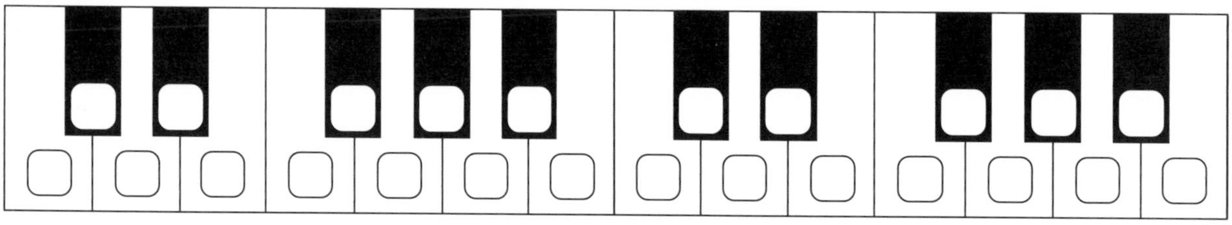

𝄢

G major

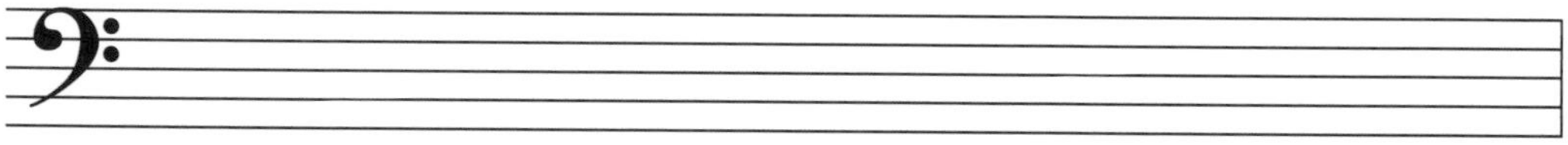

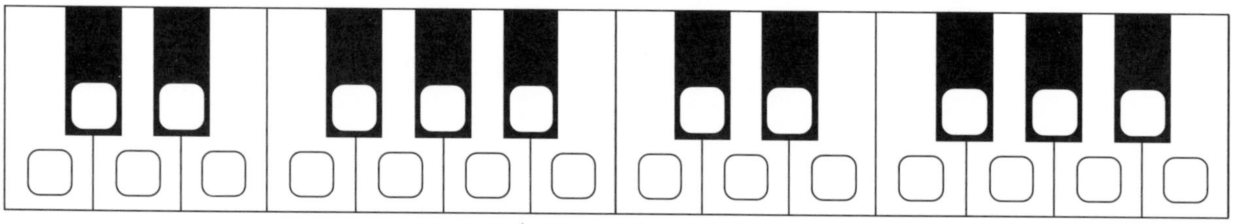

𝄢

F major

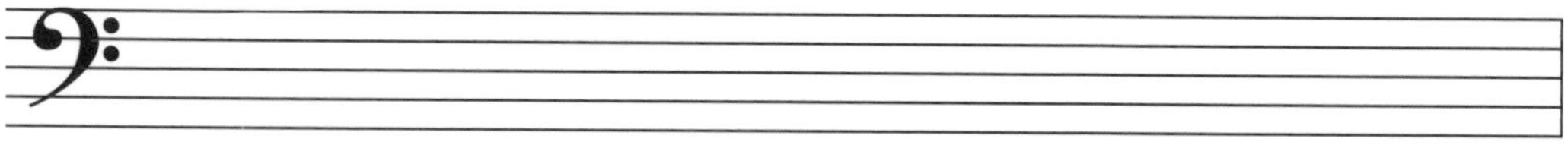

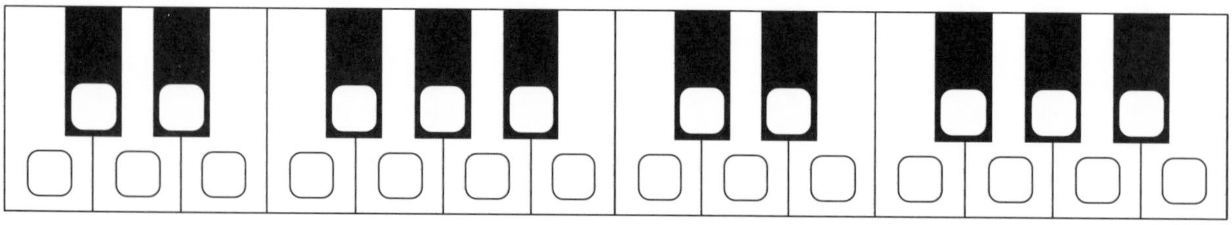

𝄢

POSITION OF STEMS

Match the boxes (Rest = R). Pay attention to the stems. Only 1 box is correct.

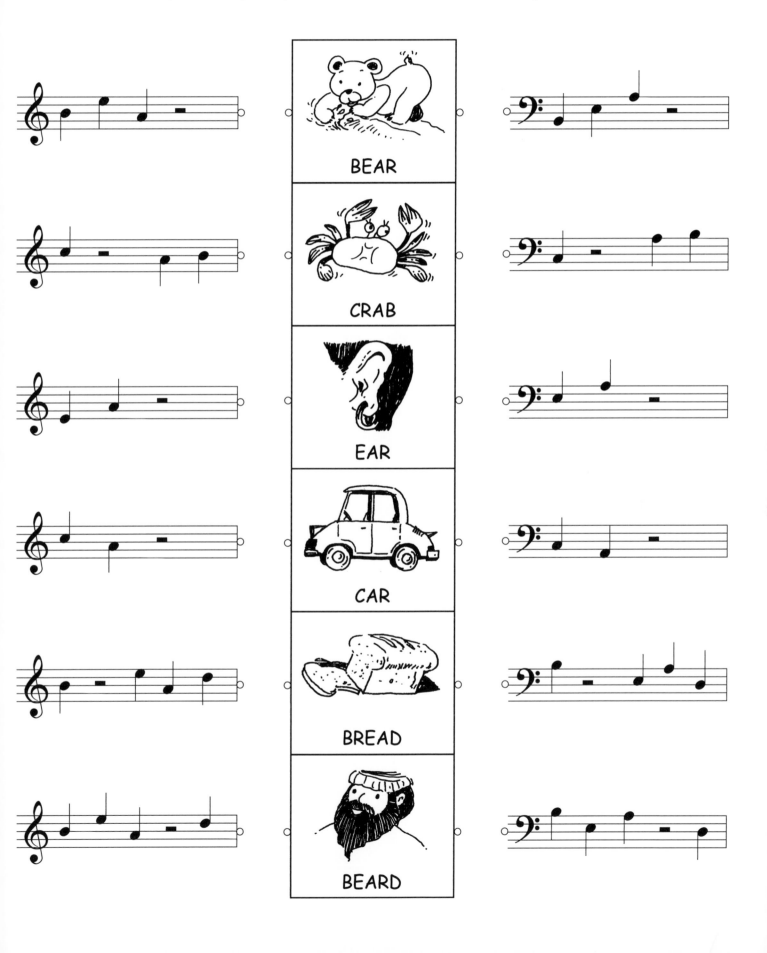

BEAR

CRAB

EAR

CAR

BREAD

BEARD

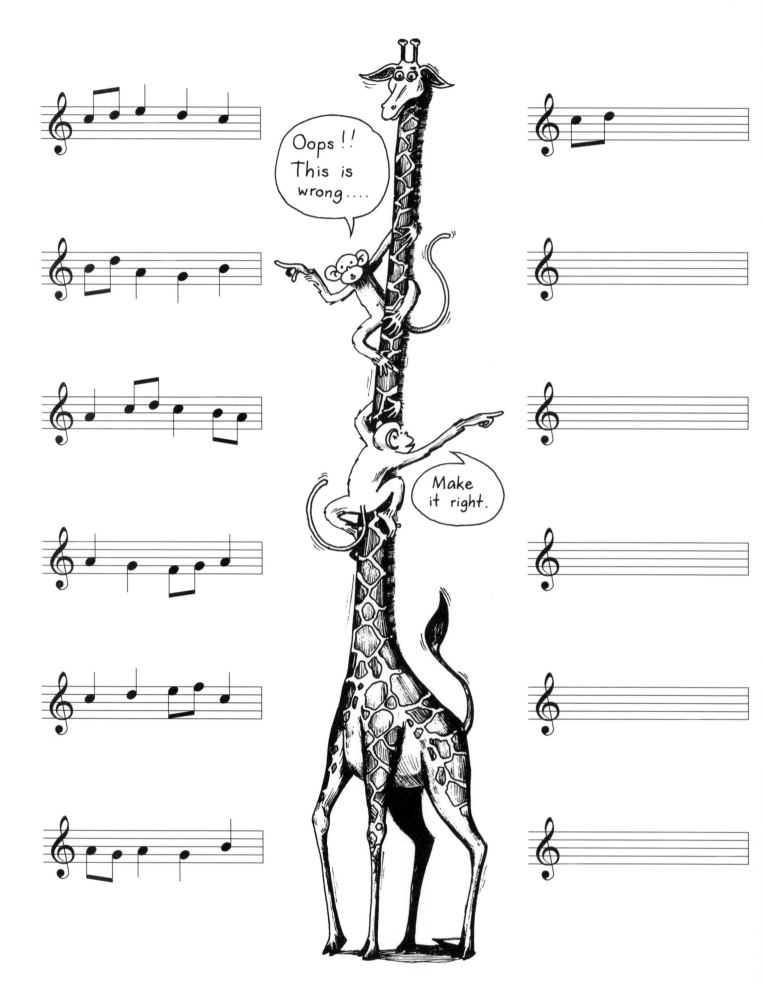

CHANGING OCTAVES

Write these notes 1 octave lower in the bass staff. Careful with the stems.

Write these notes 2 octaves lower in the bass staff.

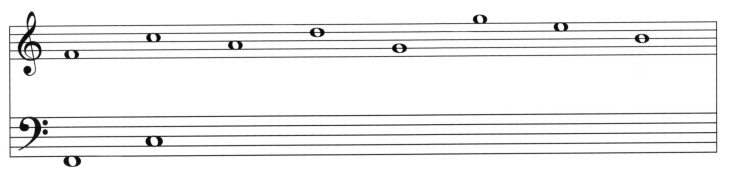

Write these notes 2 octaves higher in the treble staff.

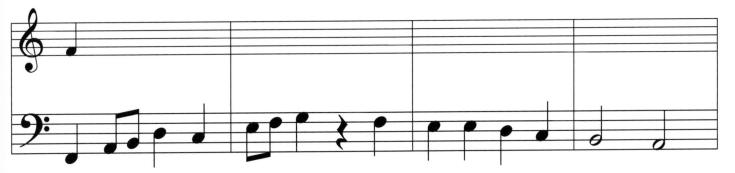

DOUBLE NOTE VALUES

Fill in the blanks.

♪ x 2 = ____   ǯ x 2 = ____

♩ x 2 = ____   𝄾 x 2 = ____

♩. x 2 = ____   ▬ x 2 = ____

𝅗𝅥 x 2 = ____

Re-write the following doubling the value of each note and rest.

HALF NOTE VALUES

Fill in the blanks.

o	÷	2	= ___		▬	÷	2	= ___
𝅗𝅥·	÷	2	= ___		▬	÷	2	= ___
𝅗𝅥	÷	2	= ___		𝄾	÷	2	= ___
♩	÷	2	= ___					

Re-write the following halving the value of each note and rest.

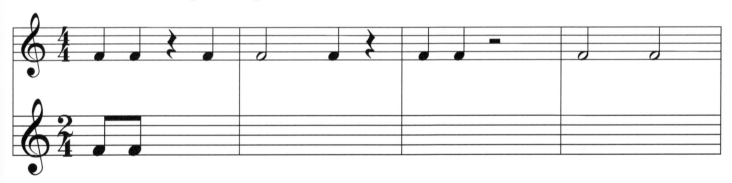

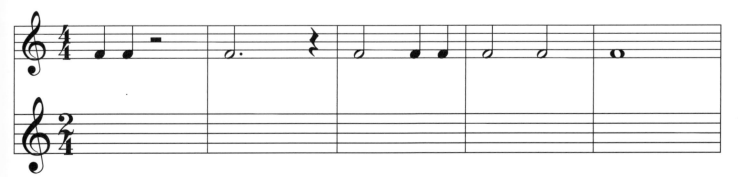

 TONIC TRIADS My

A tonic triad consists of 3 notes.
They are the **1st**, **3rd** & **5th** notes of the scale.

Circle the notes that would form a tonic triad and play the chord on the keyboard.

1) C major - Ⓒ D Ⓔ F Ⓖ A B C
              1 2 3 4 5 6 7 8

2) F major - F G A B♭ C D E F
              1 2 3 4 5 6 7 8

3) G major - G A B C D E F♯ G
              1 2 3 4 5 6 7 8

Copy the tonic triads. Start from the bottom note.

C major

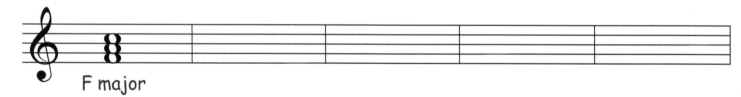

F major

G major

Write the tonic triads named.

C major   G major   F major   G major   C major

Add a note to form the tonic triad named.

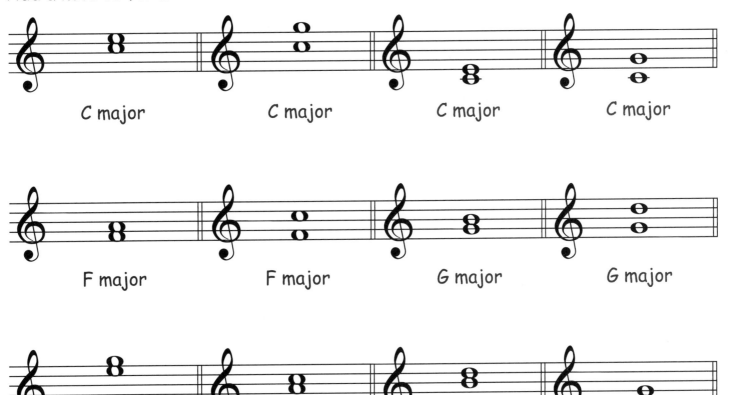

Add 2 notes to form the tonic triad named.

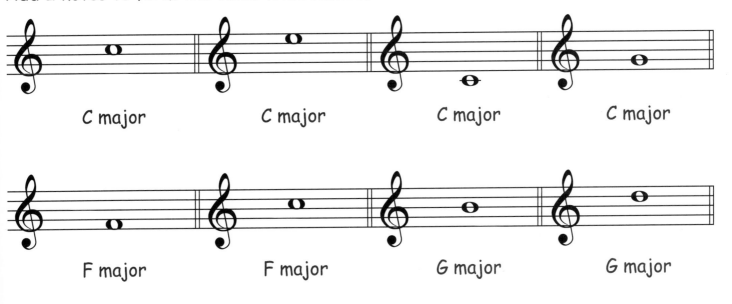

My

Beauty In The Woods

Beauty must name the 3 tonic triads before the Beast allows her home to see her father. Fill in the key of the tonic triads and the 3 notes in the correct order.

___ Major
| C | | |

___ Major
| G | | |

___ Major
| F | | |

Copy the tonic triads. Start from the bottom note.

C major

F major

G major

Write the tonic triads named.

G major   C major   F major   G major

C major   G major   C major   F major

FISHING

Come and join us on this fishing trip.

Can you name the kinds of fish in the sea?

There are 3 kinds here: C major, G major, F major.

Each of us has caught a fish.

Label on our hats the fish we have caught.

C major
| C |

G major
| G |

F major
| F |

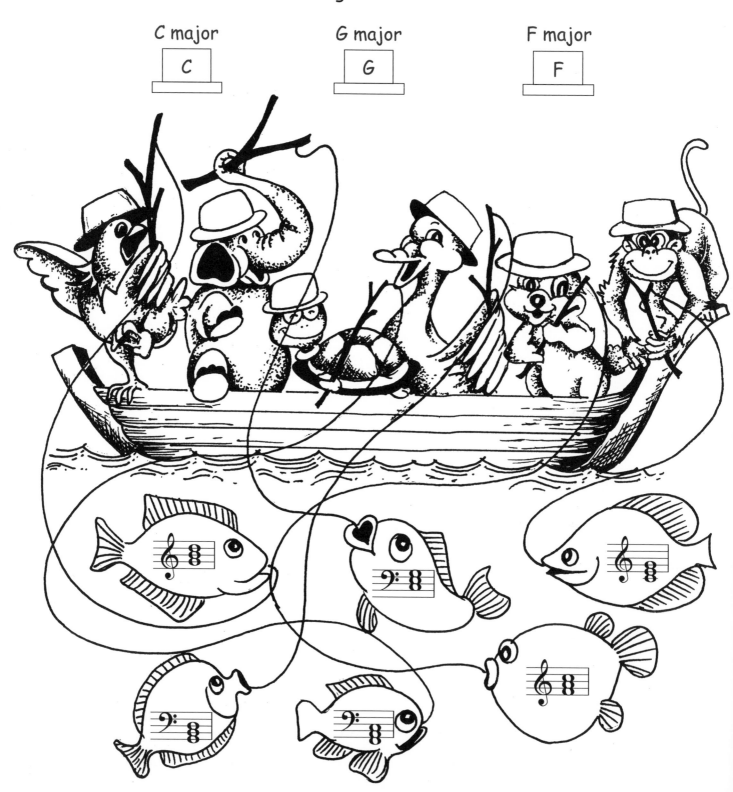

Add bar-lines.

Write notes a half step higher.

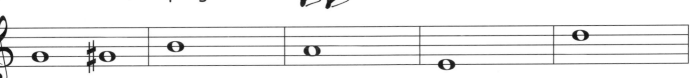

Write notes a whole step higher.

Write notes at 2 different places in the staff.

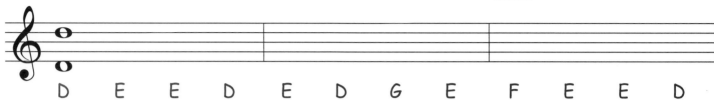

D E E D E D G E F E E D

B A G C A B F A G

Add accidentals (♯ or ♭) to indicate the key.

G major

F major

Name the key.

Key _____

Key _____

Key _____

Key _____

My

Write the notes 1 octave lower in the bass stave.

Add bar-lines to the following and name the key.

Key _____

Key _____

Key _____

TesT

My 🎼

NAME: _____

DATE: _____

1. Add bar-lines.   20

2. Write the time signature and counts.   20

3. Name the key.   20

Key _____

Key _____

Key _____

Key _____

4.   Complete the measures with rests.   20

5.   Write the tonic triads named.   10

G major   C major   F major   C major   G major

6.   Write the scales. Add the key signature and slur half steps.   10

F major (B♭)

G major (F♯)

CROSSWORD PUZZLE

My

ACROSS

1) ♯

2) 𝄞

3) 𝄽 This is a _____.

4) ♩ This is a _____ note.

5) 𝅝 This is a _____ note.

6) 𝄢 This is the bass _____.

7) ♩‿♩ This is a _____.

DOWN

1) F♯ is the key _____ of G major.

8)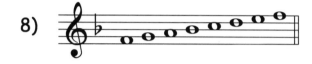

This is the _____ of F major.

9) An _____ consists of 8 notes.

10) ♩. has _____ counts.

11) ♭

12) The staff consists of _____ lines.

CROSSWORD PUZZLE

1 S

10

5 H

3 R 8 S

9

6 C 11 12 F

2 T L

7 T

4 Q E

KEY SIGNATURES

My

(2 - 4 players)

G major	- F♯
F major	- B♭
C major	- X

1. Cut out the 44 cards on the cover.

2. Put into a box.

3. Each player takes 6 cards.

4. Open 1 card to start the game. Example: G major
   The rest become the stack for drawing additional cards.

5. The 1st player opens 1 of the 3 cards.

   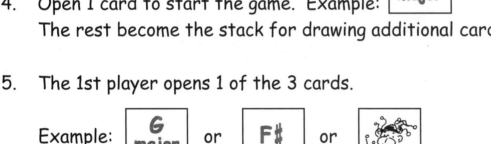

6. The 2nd, 3rd and 4th players follow.
   If a player does not have either of the 3 cards, he draws from the stack.

7. When the 4th player has opened his card, take 1 card from the stack and open. If it is a joker, change the card.

8. The player with no card left is the winner.

9. The Joker represents any card.

   If **F♯** is opened, cards that follow should be **F♯** , **G major** or **Joker**.

   If **X** is opened, cards that follow should be **X**, **C major** or **Joker**.

   If **B♭** is opened, cards that follow should be **B♭** , **F major** or **Joker**.